The
Senior's
to Dating (Again)

Traditional and Online

By Rebecca Sharp Colmer
and Todd M. Thomas

Foreword by Vera Ritchie, The Dating Coach

EKLEKTIKA PRESS
Chelsea, Michigan

The

Senior's Guide
to Dating (Again)

Traditional and Online

Check out these other great titles in the Senior's Guide Series!

The
Senior's Guide
to Digital Photography

The
Senior's Guide
to Easy Computing

The
Senior's Guide
to eBay®

To Flip

The giving of love
Is an education in itself.

Eleanor Roosevelt

FOREWORD

To have the privilege of contributing to Rebecca and Todd's book, *The Senior's Guide to Dating*, is one that I truly cherish. They are the best — each is a good writer, coach, and friend!

Over the past twenty years I have helped people develop their personal and professional skills, improve and maintain relationships and learn to utilize the best of their personality to become more successful in their endeavors. I will definitely use this book in my seminars. If you are thinking about the possibility of dating again, then this book is for you. It will take you through every stage of the process.

Remember, there is someone out there waiting to meet you. Take the next step.

Vera Ritchie, the Dating Coach
(aka Dr. Sparks!)

Table of Contents

Table of Contents

Table of Contents

Table of Contents

Table of Contents

Table of Contents

Table of Contents

DISCLAIMER

Every effort has been made to make this book as complete as possible and as accurate as possible. However, there may be mistakes both typographical and in content. Therefore, this text should be used as a general guide and not the ultimate source of information.

LIMIT OF LIABILITY/DISCLAIMER OF WARRANTY: WHILE THE PUBLISHER AND AUTHORS HAVE USED THEIR BEST EFFORTS IN PREPARING THIS BOOK, THEY MAKE NO REPRESENTATIONS OR WARRANTIES WITH RESPECT TO THE ACCURACY OR COMPLETENESS OF THE CONTENTS OF THIS BOOK AND SPECIFICALLY DISCLAIM ANY IMPLIED WARRANTIES OF MERCHANTABILITY OR FITNESS FOR A PARTICULAR PURPOSE. NO WARRANTY MAY BE CREATED OR EXTENDED BY SALES REPRESENTATIVES OR WRITTEN SALES MATERIALS. THE ADVICE AND STRATEGIES CONTAINED HEREIN MAY NOT BE SUITABLE FOR YOUR SITUATION. YOU SHOULD CONSULT WITH A PROFESSIONAL WHERE APPROPRIATE. NEITHER THE PUBLISHER NOR AUTHORS SHALL BE LIABLE FOR ANY LOSS OF PROFIT OR ANY OTHER COMMERCIAL DAMAGES, INCLUDING BUT NOT LIMITED TO SPECIAL, INCIDENTAL, CONSEQUENTIAL, OR OTHR DAMAGES.

PART 1

Welcome to Dating (Again)

... so you want to date again? Congratulations! You have taken a great first step by buying this book.

This book was written to help allay some of the fears associated with dating. Remember, dating is nothing more than getting to know someone and letting them get to know you.

Some of the old, traditional dating rituals have changed. Now we have Internet dating, speed dating and lunch dating. Don't worry; romance and chemistry are still the key ingredients.

Take it slow, keep it simple! Enjoy!

WHAT IS A DATE?

A date is when two people get together at a specified time on a certain day (with advance notice and advance planning) for the purpose of doing something special, together.

A date may be just a pleasant coming together; a way of saying thank you for a favor, or it may be a delicate step in a courtship and mating dance.

No matter how smart, rich or successful you may be, when it comes to matters of the heart, it may take awhile to develop a sense of what works for you. But the one thing that says it all about dating is: it is about communication.

Remember, "Communication" is a two way street. Don't monopolize.

WHAT ARE THE DATING STATISTICS FOR SENIORS?

Single Seniors:

- Did you know there are over 85 million unmarried adults in the United States?
- Singles make up more than 40 percent of the population. True, not all of them are seniors.
- The older population (65+) numbers over 35 million.
- About one in every eight, or 12 percent, of the population is an older American.
- There are 14.5 million unmarried and single Americans age 65 and over. These older Americans comprise 15 percent of all unmarried and single people.
- About 31 percent (9.9 million) non-institutionalized older persons are single (7.6 million women, 2.3 million men).
- Ten percent of all seniors are divorced or separated.

WHAT IS DATING LIKE IN IN
TODAY'S WORLD?

These days the trend in dating, for Seniors, is geared more for having fun and companionship rather than for casual sex or marriage. We have seen a shift in people's habits and beliefs. Current events and changes in technology may require you to update your dating style from years ago.

There is a new focus on health, well being and spirituality. Although we all remember what we could do when we were younger, we all have limitations on what we can do today.

The bottom line is that dating is supposed to be fun and enjoyable. Maybe a few butterflies will flutter in your tummy, but that is part of the thrill of dating.

HOW HAS DATING CHANGED?

Here are some ways dating may have changed since you last dated:

- There are plenty of ways to meet new people, some modern, some traditional. Today, there are dating and matchmaking services, singles functions, and the Internet.
- Women ask men out.
- The time for dates has changed. These days, coffee dates and lunch dates are popular.
- Men and women are more open about sex.
- More people are divorced.

HOW HAS DATING STAYED THE SAME?

Although some aspects of dating have changed, much of it remains the same. The following list will remind you of ways in which it has stayed the same:

- There are still anxieties and challenges associated with dating.
- All the "good ones" are not taken.
- It is important to keep an open mind about who is right for you.
- Personal growth is the key to successful dating.
- Creating and maintaining healthy relationships takes some work.
- It's fun to meet new people!

WHICH IS BETTER, TRADITIONAL OR ONLINE DATING?

There is no one perfect way to date. You will develop your own individual style and strategy. Potential dates are everywhere!

Some of you will prefer to meet others by joining a club, visiting museums and art galleries, poetry readings, taking group tours, going to singles resorts...and the list goes on and on.

Some of you will prefer a faster and more streamlined approach by using the Internet or a dating service. Some of you will incorporate a little of both.

Regardless of how you approach the dating world, remember to have fun. Enjoy yourself!

ARE THERE DIFFERENT LEVELS
OF DATING?

Yes. There are two ways to look at dating:
casual or serious. Ask yourself these questions:

- Are you looking for someone to join you for
  dinner, go to the theatre or just spend some
  time with or are you looking for a partner in
  the sexual arena?
- Are you looking for a marriage partner, a
  long term relationship or just companionship?

DO I NEED A DATING PLAN?

The truth is that to date successfully, you need to take charge of your dating life. Start with a plan.

First, make the decision to start your dating search.

Second, you need a good self image. Make sure that you view yourself as desirable to others. Make any self-improvements needed to put forth a good image.

Lastly, do some research about where you are most likely to find the types of people you are hoping to meet. Then, get out there and start meeting people. Don't hesitate to enlist others to help you in your quest.

AM I TOO OLD TO DATE?

No. Wanting a partner is not a character flaw. In fact, it's perfectly natural. No matter what your age or social circumstance, you don't have to apologize for actively looking for the absolute best partner for you.

You may have been married before. Some Seniors report feeling a little guilty at first, about dating, as if that disparages the memory of your past loved one.

This is just another time in your life and you should enjoy it to the fullest. If that means sharing it with someone else, there is no reason to have any guilt feelings.

IS IT OKAY TO DATE MORE THAN ONE PERSON AT A TIME?

Dating is something you do before making binding choices or exclusive commitments. Dating involves choices. You have the right to choose, or not to choose to be with someone.

You do not have to date just one person until it's "dump them" or "marry them" time.

You may find that certain dates make going out to dinner more enjoyable, but others make a concert more fun.

It's probably best to date a few people before you make any personal commitments.

WHAT IF MY CHILDREN THINK I SHOULDN'T DATE?

You are entitled to date and love again — at any age or under any circumstance.

Be happy that your kids don't want you to get hurt, or are just looking out for you. But hey! They're kids! What do they know? "They should be seen, and not heard." Okay, listen to them, nod your head and smile, and go date anyway!

Your kids have a life, why not you? Just don't spring it on them. Be sure to include them in on your decision.

PART 2

Personal Inventory

Now that you are about to enter the dating world, it is a good time to take a personal inventory. You will have a much more successful and pleasant dating experience if you know who you are and what you want.

Learn to love yourself and to accept your "unique" self. If you like who you are and are confident in yourself, others will be attracted to you.

WHY SHOULD I TAKE A PERSONALITY ASSESSMENT?

Why not? The first step toward finding out the best kind of date for you is figuring out what kind of date you are.

To learn about your personality style, visit www.DrRohm.com and take a personality assessment. You will get a report of over 40 pages about your personal style. This is an excellent way to update your "personal inventory".

ARE MY DATING EXPECTATIONS REALISTIC?

One of the biggest problems with dating is that each person may have different expectations when they date. Some people want a good time and nothing more. Some people expect a commitment from the first date. It is important to always be honest — with yourself and with your date.

When we date we tend to show our best side. Over time our "real" self will be fully revealed. This is a normal occurrence in the dating process and should not be pushed.

Be prepared for compromise. However, know in your heart what is truly important to you.

WHAT IF I DO NOT FEEL SELF-CONFIDENT?

Even if you do not feel very confident, it is important that you appear confident. You can make confidence a habit just like any other habit.

You have to learn to trust yourself. Take time to evaluate your positive qualities. You will find that there are many more than you may think. Each day, you should look over your small successes and use them to reinforce your confidence.
Keep in mind that it is perfectly natural to feel a little insecure about meeting new people. Most people, regardless of age, feel a little vulnerable when dating.

We get asked, "How are you?" all the time — even from strangers. You should always respond positively even if you are not feeling positive.
Try to use some of these responses:

- Great!
- Getting better everyday.
- Loving life, having fun.
- Marvelous.

FIVE QUESTIONS TO ASK BEFORE DATING

It may have been a long time since you last dated. Just the thought of dating can be both exciting and terrifying. It's understandable to have some fears associated with dating. A good way to start the dating process is to ask yourself a few questions such as:

1. Do I really want to date?
2. Why do I want to date?
3. Do I know who I am?
4. Do I know who I am looking for?
5. Why should someone be looking for me?

WHAT IF I HAVE DATING FEARS?

Everyone who dates usually feels stress or anxiety, at least occasionally. Some of the most common fears are:

- What if I do not find anyone?
- What if I get rejected?
- What if I do not like my date?
- What if my date does not like me?
- What if I say or do the wrong thing?
- What if I feel totally out of place?
- What if I get a disease?
- What if I fall in love?

Part of the thrill of dating is getting past those fears so you can get to know someone and they can get to know you.

HOW SHOULD I HANDLE DATING FEARS?

Relax. Look at dating fears this way; if you are fearful, even though you know that you are a great catch, think about how the other person feels! Your date probably has the same fears and insecurities as you.

Take a deep breath and face your fears. Don't be controlled by your fears. Dating should be fun and not stressful.

If you feel really nervous or fearful, tell your date. You may find that your date is nervous too. Acknowledging your fears can help to put you at ease.

Relax and enjoy the experience.

ISN'T DATING LIKE A GAME?

No, dating is not a game. There are no winners and losers. Dating is a learning experience that should allow both people to grow.

Don't pretend to be the person your date is looking for, if you're not. Don't pretend to be somebody you are not.

Also, be honest about your past. Equally as important, be honest about what you want for the future and the relationship.

WHAT IF I HAVE A MEDICAL CONDITION OR HANDICAP?

This is a very important topic that should be discussed more often. Depending on your condition, you may have some limitations on what you can do while dating. Don't look at your condition as an impediment to meeting new people.

Also, do not hide any medical condition from a potential date if it affects the way *you* feel about going out. Be open and honest, it will make you and your date feel more relaxed.

WHAT IF I AM UNATTRACTIVE?

You are only as unattractive as you feel. Chances are that your date feels unattractive as well.

Don't worry, love is blind. Put your best self forward. A healthy self-esteem is the ultimate sex appeal. If your prospective date cannot see past your "shell", then you know they have an unattractive inside.

Being overly self-conscious about your appearance can sabotage your dating success. Remember, everyone's body changes as we age.

Beauty is in the eye of the beholder and that's the one you are looking for.

WHAT ABOUT LONELINESS?

Don't let loneliness cloud your good judgment about dating. In fact, before you start dating, it is a good idea to "warm up" a bit by participating in larger get-togethers — cruises, parties, large social functions, religious functions.

Go out to concerts, movies or art galleries. Go by yourself or go out with a friend.

Go be social, because anyone who wants to go out with you will want you to be a social person.

ARE YOU SET IN YOUR WAYS?

Seniors are usually the first to admit that they are set in their ways. By now you probably know what works for you and what you want in life.

Remember, dating is about meeting new people and learning about *them*. It is important to realize that if you are set in your ways, most likely so are the people you meet. Practice being flexible and understanding.

No one wants to be told that the way they do something is wrong.

ARE THERE TIMES WHEN IT IS BETTER NOT TO DATE?

It is a good idea to postpone dating if:

- You are clinically depressed and "need" to find someone rather than "want" to find someone.
- Immediately following the death of a spouse, parent, friend or anybody you feel close to.
- You have just lost a place to live and you are not sure where you will go next.
- You don't feel like dating.

WHAT IF I'M NOT GOOD WITH PEOPLE, IN GENERAL?

Try to look at dating with a new perspective — one that is open-minded and optimistic. It is natural to dread a new dating experience if you have had a bad one.

Remember, over the years you have grown emotionally. You can overcome your fears and get excited about dating.

Keep in mind that you cannot control how your date will act or respond, but you can control your own actions and responses.

PART 3

Finding People

By now you have looked at who you are and you know what you want. Now it is time to develop some new friendships. How do you even begin to meet people, particularly those who share the same interests as you? In the beginning it may seem rather daunting. Don't worry it will get easier.

The Internet has added a new dimension to meeting people. It's a great communication tool. Just as the telephone did, over a hundred years ago, the Internet is allowing people to connect, who otherwise may never have without it.

WHAT'S THE BEST WAY TO MEET PEOPLE?

If you are not sure you are ready to jump into the dating scene, why not focus on making new friends? There are probably lots of folks in your own area who are looking for someone to share a good conversation, a hobby or lunch.

Once you get used to meeting new people and making friends, it is much easier to start looking for a date. It is also easier to add to your circle of friends rather than adopting a totally new circle of friends.

Expand your social network. Invite your friends to invite their friends when going out. Chances are you will make a new friend who could easily turn into a date.

WHERE CAN I FIND POTENTIAL DATES?

It is important to remain open to new opportunities. Get into the habit of speaking to at least three new people each day, whether at the grocery store, in an elevator or at the doctor's office.

It doesn't matter the person's age when you meet. Most importantly, it's the process of meeting and talking to new people. Everyone you meet doesn't have to be a potential date. Besides, every young person knows someone in your age range!

HOW DO I OVERCOME SHYNESS?

With a little practice you can overcome your shyness and gain self-confidence. Here are some things to practice:

- Practice smiling and making eye contact.
- Say hello to everyone you pass on the street or in a corridor.
- Shake hands and introduce yourself to new people.
- Answer the phone with some spunkiness in your voice.
- Regardless of how you feel, when asked how you are, always answer, "Great!"
- Smile.

TEN WAYS TO MEET NEW PEOPLE

Get into the habit of enjoying life and not just looking for dates. There are plenty of places right in your own community where you can meet new people. Here are a few places to start:

- Join a health club.
- Check out museums, local parks, historical sites and libraries.
- Walk your dog, or just walk everyday at a park or place where other seniors gather.
- Go to seminars. Learn something new and make new friends with similar interests.
- Get involved in local politics.
- Join an investment club.
- Join a business or professional association.
- Attend or host community events and parties.
- Volunteer.
- Go shopping.

IS IT OKAY TO BE PROACTIVE?

Yes. You will improve your chances of meeting someone if you do something or go somewhere you enjoy. You will automatically meet people who share your interests. If you are in a place where you feel comfortable it is much easier to find something to talk about with a stranger.

You will meet more people out of your home, apartment or condo, than waiting for someone to knock on your door.

Take your household mail or paperwork, favorite book or magazine and get busy in places where you have the chance to meet people. Try the local coffee shop, hotel lobby or bar restaurant.

WHERE ELSE CAN I MEET PEOPLE?

Another way to maximize your chances of meeting new people and having fun is to always be looking for unusual places to run into interesting people. Go to new places and try new things.

- Go to as many parties as you are invited to.
- Go to an author book signing.
- Anywhere there is food: restaurants, street fairs, grocery stores.
- Bridge or other card game groups.
- Cruises.
- Home and garden shows.
- Library.
- Investment seminar.
- Start your own book review club. Ask everyone to bring a friend.
- Volunteer where you can meet people your age.

WHERE CAN I MEET PEOPLE WHO ENJOY MUSIC?

Take advantage of your hobbies to meet people.
If you enjoy music, go to musical places.
Most of the people there will share a common
interest and starting a conversation will be easy.
Consider going to these music oriented events:

- Concerts.
- Classes.
- Music Store.
- Local clubs.
- Community park recitals.
- Your grandkids' recitals.

Almost every community newspaper has
a "What's Happening" section. It may be a
monthly or weekly publication and the focus
may be for a younger crowd. However, you will
find out what is going on in your area.

WHERE CAN I MEET PEOPLE WHO ENJOY SPORTS?

You don't actually have to be a member of the team to meet others who enjoy sports. You can become a booster or just a casual observer. Check out some of these places:

- Health Clubs.
- Tennis or Golf Lessons.
- YMCAs.
- Teams on local schools and colleges.
- Professional Sporting Events.
- Bowling Leagues.
- Boating.

WHERE CAN I MEET PEOPLE WHO ENJOY SPIRITUAL OR RELIGIOUS EXPLORATION?

Most members of the following organizations report being healthier and happier than average folks:

- Yoga Classes.
- Trips to Holy Places.
- Holistic Health Fairs.
- Churches, Synagogues, Mosques.
- Philosophy classes.
- Prayer Groups.
- Bible Classes.
- Volunteer Groups.

If you are looking for a long lasting relationship, people with compatible beliefs tend to have stronger relationships.

WHERE CAN I MEET PEOPLE WHO ENJOY INTELLECTUAL PURSUITS?

You are never too old to learn something new. While you are expanding your brainpower you might just meet someone new. Consider attending some of the following:

- Lectures.
- Book Clubs.
- Personal Development Courses.
- Community College.
- Adult Continuing Education.
- Audit University Courses.

SHOULD I GO ON A BLIND DATE?

Yes! Your friends are one of the most important resources you have in meeting new people. It's quite a compliment when your friends want you to meet someone else they know. Plus, it's nice to be set-up with someone that has already been "checked out" by someone you know and trust.

If it doesn't work out, do not blame the matchmaker. Be sure to let them try again if the first blind date is not successful.

SIX TIPS ON GETTING A BLIND DATE

To get other people to set up you up on a date you've got to let them know you're available and willing. Consider these suggestions when looking for help from friends or family:

1. Put the word out that you would like to be fixed up.
2. Tell your friends or family the kind of person you'd like to meet.
3. Tell them not to make you sound desperate.
4. Ask them not to reveal too much information about you.
5. Tell them that after the date you don't want to be interrogated.
6. Promise not to hold them accountable if the date doesn't go well.

WHAT IS SPEED DATING®?

Speed Dating® was created by Los Angeles Rabbi Yaacov Deyo, in 1999. It is group matchmaking at its best. It is a way for serious daters to quickly evaluate potential partners.

There are companies all over the country that sponsor different types of Speed Dating®. Dating sessions usually run from three to ten minutes, and you can meet up to twenty people in one session. The costs are minimal.

HOW DOES SPEED DATING WORK?

Here's how it works:

1. An equal number of single women and men gather at a café or sitting area where each table is numbered. You are given a number and/or a name tag.
2. You will have three to ten minutes to chat with each potential date. Sometimes the dating company gives you suggested topics to discuss.
3. At the end of the time, a bell rings to let you know it is time to change candidates. Before you move on, you are asked to fill out a form if you would like to see this person again. Usually it is a simple form, check yes or no. Usually the ladies stay seated and the man moves to a new table.
4. After a certain time, there is a short break where you get to enjoy beverages and appetizers. This is a great time to mingle with those you have your eye on.
5. At the end of the session, the host company collects all of the forms. If both sides check off the "yes" box, then they notify the participants within two days, and give them the contact information.

ABOUT SPEED DATING AND
SIMILAR PROGRAMS

Remember, Speed Dating® is just like online dating in that you are meeting a stranger. You only have three to ten minutes to decide if you would consider this person for a date. Spend your time wisely by asking the right questions. Start out with these:

- What is/was your occupation?
- What are two important things I should know about you?
- Did you go to college? Where?
- Are you religious? What faith?
- Have you ever been married? Kids? Grandkids?
- What are your hobbies?

WHAT ARE THE ADVANTAGES OF USING A DATING SERVICE?

Using a dating service gives you a chance to expand your dating world. It is a speedier and more efficient form of blind dating or dating via personal ads.

For example, if you attend a Senior Sparks Coffee Date session, you are given a chance to look at and learn about the person that you will be dating. You will also read a profile of that individual, which tells you what the other person is looking for.

When using a dating service, most of the work is done for you. All you have to do is register, show up and pay for the introduction. Keep in mind, the reason you are doing this is to meet new people!

HOW DO I FIND A DATING SERVICE IN MY AREA?

To find a dating service in your area check the yellow pages or search online. For example, Senior Sparks offers a variation of speed dating. It's called Senior Sparks Coffee Dates. (Senior Sparks also offers an online dating service.)

It offers two kinds of introductions:

1. Introductions to Seniors looking for a date.
2. Introductions to Seniors looking to meet a friend.

You can contact their web site to request a social in your area. Their web address is: www.seniorsparks.com.

PART 4

Asking For A First Date

Now it's time to make your move. You have found someone you find attractive. You would like to go out on a date with them. It's time to advance to the next part of your game plan.

What is the best approach? What's the best way to ask for a date? In this section you will learn some ways to make the first encounter easier.

HOW DO I PREPARE FOR "THAT FIRST CALL"?

It's smart to steel yourself for a rejection to your invitation because the person you ask out may very well be busy, or already in a relationship, or may not want to go out with you. That is not a serious kind of rejection. It happens to everyone, not just to you. However, don't ask for a date with only rejection in your mind. After all, they might say yes!

Three rules for askers:

- Hope for the best: they say yes.
- Prepare for the worst: they say no.
- Expect the unexpected: they say they want to take you to Paris for dinner!

Three rules for askees:

- Go and hope for the best.
- Go for the experience.
- Have a great dinner in Paris!

IS THERE REALLY SOMEONE OUT THERE FOR ME?

Yes! If you keep scanning the entire sea with your eyes, you will appreciate all the fish swimming by, and you won't have set your sights and hopes on just one of them.

Not everyone you meet or go out on a date with will be a good match for you. Some will be great dinner companions. Others will be fun to go to concerts with. Others you will not want to date again.

And keep in mind, in your date's eyes you're just one of many fishes in the sea.

WHAT CONSTITUTES A GOOD DATE?

Everybody has different views on what makes a good date.

Some place a lot of emphasis on the person. A good date might be with a person that:

- Makes you laugh.
- Asks your opinions.
- Doesn't try to mold you.

Or a good date might depend on the activity, such as something:

- Where you can learn about each other.
- That you can enjoy.
- Where you can laugh.
- Where you can be yourself.

Most will say, "A good date is being with someone who is organized, who is a good conversationalist, who makes me think I'm special, and who puts me at ease."

WHO SHOULD DO THE "ASKING OUT"?

Have the rules changed? Yes. These days it is perfectly acceptable for the lady to ask out the gentleman. If you want to have a date with someone, ask.

If you look at the statistics again (page 17), single women outnumber single men. So ladies, if you want to go out with him, you had better ask before someone else does!

WHAT'S THE BEST WAY TO ASK
FOR A DATE?

It seems simple enough, but it can be the most difficult part of the date. Think ahead. Have a plan. You shouldn't wait until the last moment to think of what you will say when asking out someone.

Keep the "asking" casual and fun.

It is best to have a specific activity in mind for your date. For example, some of your options might include going out for coffee, going to a concert, etc.

HOW CAN I IMPROVE MY CHANCES WHEN ASKING FOR A DATE?

Get to the purpose of the call. Ask for the date. Find out what would be a good time, place and day for you to meet. Remember:

- Be yourself.
- Be casual.
- Be creative.
- After you ask for the date, don't make that the last thing you talk about.
- Always call or email when you say you will.
- Always call or email after a meeting to keep the contact going.

TWO WAYS NOT TO ASK SOMEONE
FOR A DATE

Just as there are certain ways to ask someone out for a date, there are certain ways not to ask someone out for a date. For example:

- Do not ask, "You want to go out?" It is too open-ended and can lead to an awkward follow-up conversation.
- Do not ask, "What are you doing on Friday night?" It's too vague. It may leave your potential date wondering exactly what you have in mind.

WHEN IS IT TIME TO MOVE ON?

If you make three attempts to make a date and get turned down each time, move on. More than likely the person is sending you a message. (Some people have as much a problem giving rejection as receiving it.)

If you get rejected, try it again with somebody else. It's like falling off a horse: you have to get back in the saddle.

If you think you are getting too many rejections, it could be time to take a closer look at your style. You may need to re-evaluate your approach.

HOW TO GET A PHONE NUMBER OR E-MAIL ADDRESS?

Discuss something interesting and then suggest that you exchange numbers/e-mails for further discussion.

Or, you can always take the direct approach and just ask for their phone number or e-mail address.

It helps if you have a name card or business card to hand out with all of your contact information on it.

IS IT OKAY TO ASK FOR A FIRST DATE FOR A WEEKEND NIGHT?

Save the weekend dates for later in the dating process. Weekend dates are considered "big" date nights. Even people who haven't had a date in years are hesitant to admit they have weekend nights open.

However, if weekends are the only time you can go out, or if your prospective date is limited to weekends only, ignore this advice.

SHOULD I TRY THE OPEN-ENDED INVITATION APPROACH?

An old sales technique is to never ask a question in which the person can easily answer no and shut down the work process. When asking for a date, try and phrase your request with some specifics.

For example, it's not a good idea to ask, "Would you like to go out sometime?" It's better to ask, "Let's go for coffee on Thursday?"

WHAT ARE SOME WAYS TO ASK FOR A DATE?

The best way to ask for a date is to ask in person, face to face. The good news and the bad news is you get an immediate response!

You can also ask by phone. This way they cannot see you sweat! However, you usually get less information because you cannot read their body language.

You can ask by e-mail. However, there is the chance the invitation can be delayed or "lost".

You can ask by a hand-written note. Resist the urge to send the note with flowers, cigars or any gift. You don't want to appear that you are trying to bribe them.

WHAT IF I GET AN ANSWERING MACHINE WHEN I CALL?

Okay, you have finally gotten up your nerve to make the call, to ask for a date and the person isn't home. You get the answering machine instead.

Never ask for a date on an answering machine. It's better to just leave your name and that you will try to reach them later. The worst thing you can do is to hang up without a brief message. It is okay to ask them to return your call.

PART 5

First Dates

First dates are a necessary evil in the lives of singles. With all the high hopes, expectations and fears that come with a first date, it's a wonder anyone makes it to a second date!

Above all, relax, enjoy yourself.

Asking someone out for a first date is actually the second hardest thing to do. The hardest thing is asking for the second date. Now you're going to find out how much they liked the first one!

WHAT IF FEAR IS RUINING MY GOOD ATTITUDE?

Make sure that you have the right mindset. A date is a way to get to know someone. You should plan on having a good experience. Keep it simple. It is only one date, not a lifelong commitment.

Remind yourself that your date already likes something about you or they would have said no. Don't worry about what will happen if things don't work out. Enjoy the moment.

PRE-DATE MAKEOVER

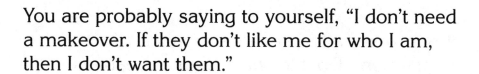

You are probably saying to yourself, "I don't need a makeover. If they don't like me for who I am, then I don't want them."

Settle down. What we mean is to look as wonderful as you possibly can and make sure that you have a good attitude.

You only get one chance to make a first impression. Obviously you made a good one prior to asking them out or you would not be going out on a date.

You only get to have one "first date" with this person. You want to make a great first date impression.

HOW DO I MAKE A GOOD FIRST DATE IMPRESSION?

It only takes a few seconds to make a first impression. Double check your appearance checklist:

- Be comfortable with your weight.
- Hair neat and trimmed. If not, get a haircut.
- Clean teeth and good breath.
- Update your wardrobe.
- Clean your fingernails.
- Wear clean shoes.
- Be clean-body and hair.
- Remove any stray nostril or ear hair.

Some things, such as weight loss or fixing your teeth, may take some time to accomplish. Don't wait to start dating while you're making changes.

As a matter of fact, why not put on your "first date impression" even before you start looking for someone to ask out.

HAVE A SENSE OF HUMOR

The best way to make a good impression on a first date is to keep your sense of humor. People who try too hard to be charming can become very uptight when things go wrong. And things will go wrong.

Having a sense of humor is not about telling jokes. It's about how you view, and react to, what transpires around you.

DOS AND DON'TS ON A FIRST DATE

Remember, the purpose of the first date is to get to know your date and to decide if you want a second date.

Dos:

- Be your best self.
- Be a good listener.
- Have fun and lighten up.
- Be honest.
- Smile.
- Address your date by name.

Don'ts:

- Pretend to be someone you're not.
- Bring up all of your vulnerabilities and insecurities.
- Lie.
- Become intoxicated.
- Make unwanted advances.

HOW DO I PICK THE RIGHT ACTIVITY FOR THE FIRST DATE?

The right activity depends upon what you and your date have in common. If you share a similar interest such as bridge, go to a bridge party. If you don't have a lot in common, go to lunch or for coffee.

Pick something that you would like to do. This will guarantee that at least one person will have a good time! Also, pick something that you can afford. Don't "spend to impress".

Also, pick an activity that doesn't require you to buy new clothes. One of the keys to successful first dates is being comfortable. Be comfortable in what you wear, where you go and what you do.

IS IT OKAY TO HAVE SOME FRIENDLY COMPETITION ON THE FIRST DATE?

On a first date, it's probably not a good idea to engage in an activity where there is a winner and a loser. Let's face it, some people are not gracious losers or gracious winners!

Stay on neutral turf. Often it's not easy to put competitive feelings in the right context.

MOVIE FIRST DATES: PROS AND CONS

The movie theatre is a safe place to go for a first date. However, you really cannot get to know someone during the movie as you should not be talking. If you talk during the movie you risk getting thrown out. That's a bad thing!

Of course, after the movie, or before, you could arrange to go some place for dessert or coffee.

ARE THERE ANY FIRST DATES
I SHOULD AVOID?

Of course there are exceptions to every rule, but generally, avoid the following for first dates:

- Weddings.
- New Year's Eve.
- Thanksgiving or Christmas.
- Valentine's Day.
- Beach.

HOW MUCH TIME SHOULD BE SPENT ON THE FIRST DATE?

Keep it short, a couple of hours at the most. You can learn enough about the person in a few hours that will determine if it's worth spending more time together.

Plan your time wisely. There is nothing worse than being stuck in an unpleasant situation.

WHO PAYS ON THE FIRST DATE?

The person who asks, pays. However, even if the woman does the asking it would behoove the man to pay for the date (or at least offer). Some things never go out of style.

After the first date, it's perfectly fine to offer to "Go Dutch" or take turns paying for the date.

ADDITIONAL ITEMS FOR MAKING A GOOD FIRST IMPRESSION

Checklist:

- Dress appropriately and comfortably.
- No perfume or cologne — just in case they are allergic to it.
- Good hygiene-clean hair, clean ears (inside and out), teeth brushed, nails clipped/filed, shave)
- Arrive on time.
- Good conversation.
- Don't overstay your welcome. You want them to ask you back, rather than ask you to leave.

WHAT IF I'M NOT A GOOD COVERSATIONALIST?

Because everybody is nervous in the beginning, start with some small talk. Give your date a compliment.

Talk about subjects that are meaningful to both you and your date. Ask questions and be sure to listen to the answers in order to find out their interests. The best conversationalists are not the ones who talk the most, but rather those who listen the most.

Also, try to stay positive rather than negative. Be careful not to ramble on and on. Let your date give their opinions, too.

Ask for feedback.

ARE THERE ANY TABOO TOPICS ON A FIRST DATE?

Stay away from the following topics:

- Sex.
- Ex-spouses.
- Politics.
- Religion.
- Previous date experiences.

IS TMI (TOO MUCH INFORMATION) A PROBLEM?

Resist the temptation to bare your soul on the first date. There is a time and place for everything.

Leave the following at home:

- Vulnerabilities.
- Anxieties.
- Fears.
- Baggage.
- Insecurities.
- Skeletons.
- Stupidities (If you catch yourself droning on and on about yourself, ask forgiveness from your date, and then stop!).

WHAT DO I NEED TO KNOW ABOUT BODY LANGUAGE?

Your body speaks louder than words. Stay observant.

- Occasional Nodding: You're on the same wavelength.
- Continuous Nodding: You've lost the connection.
- Relaxed Posture: Indicates your date is open and non-defensive.
- Palms Up: Indicates warm and receptive heart.
- Arms Behind the Head: Classic sign of dominance, or attempting to gain it.
- Mirroring: Unconsciously reflecting each other's behavior — attuned to each other.
- Arms Crossed: Indicates a barrier between the two of you.
- Yawning: Bored.

There are a number of books regarding the signals we all send through body language.

Avoid: Scratching any private body parts.

ARE THERE ANY FIRST DATE RED FLAGS?

Not all red flags are the same. Some you can live with, others will make you run the other way, and others will just drive you crazy. Things to consider:

- Rudeness or moodiness.
- Late for the date.
- Tells lies.
- Talks too much about sex or money.
- Tells too many jokes.
- Talks too much (in general).
- Doesn't talk at all.
- Complains too much.
- Sloppy, dirty clothes, or un-shined shoes.
- Poor table manners.
- Chain smokes or drinks alcohol excessively.

Men: Make sure your fly is zipped.

Women: Check your blouse to be sure all the buttons are in the correct holes.

TO KISS OR NOT KISS?

Read your date's body language to tell if he/she is open to being touched at all. Be sensitive about personal boundaries.

Often it is best to start out with a good hand-shake, firm, but not too tight or to try a hug to test responsiveness. Build up to a kiss on the lips by starting with a kiss on the cheek.

Remember, you want to be asked to return, not to leave. Be cautious, but also don't be scared.

WHAT'S THE BEST WAY TO END A DATE?

If you are both having a good time, you can always extend the date. If you have an inkling that things are not going well, don't prolong it. Just end it promptly.

Follow these suggestions to end your date:

- Don't say you'll call unless you mean it.
- Say thank you.
- Come right out and ask if there will be a second date, if you want one. Try this, *"May I see you again — next week perhaps?"* If you have a personal (social) card, offer it.
- If you had a great time, don't be afraid to say it.
- If you are not interested in another date, find something nice to say without making any references to a future get-together.

PART 6

Dating Safety and Etiquette

There was a time when dating was simple. Men were expected to be gentlemen and women were expected to be ladies. Their roles were clear-cut. There was not so much chaos in the world and it was a lot easier to stay safe.

This section introduces you to some standard dating precautions and a few of the "new" dating rules.

WHAT IS THE BEST SAFETY TOOL?

Whether you decide to date the old-fashioned way or online, please use sound judgment and be responsible for your conduct. In both the virtual and real worlds, common sense is your best safety tool.

As much as we would like everyone else to be as open and honest as we are, it might not be so with your next date. Let them earn your trust with their words and deeds.

Exercising careful, thoughtful decisions will help yield better dating results.

SHOULD I SCREEN MY DATES?

When you first meet someone new, do not hesitate to ask about his/her background. In fact, it's a good idea to reshape some of your questions just to make sure there are no holes in their story. If you discover any discrepancies it is a good idea to steer clear of this potential date.

Trust your instincts. If anything makes you feel uncomfortable, walk away for your own protection.

WHAT IF MY DATE SEEMS TOO GOOD TO BE TRUE?

Watch out for someone who seems too good to be true. Begin by good communication, and then look out for odd behavior or inconsistencies. The person at the other end of the phone or Internet may not be who or what he or she claims.

Con artists come in all shapes, sizes and ages. If the hairs on the back of your neck start sticking up, be very careful.

Stay alert, pay attention, and follow your intuition.

SHOULD I TELL SOMEONE WHERE I AM GOING ON MY DATE?

Yes. Always let someone know where you are going and with whom, and when you expect to be home.

If you are going to be later than you first thought, call them so they do not worry.

WHAT IF I DON'T KNOW MY DATE'S LAST NAME?

You would be surprised to know how many people go on a first date without knowing their date's last name or how to spell it. Don't be afraid to ask. Write it down on a piece of paper and keep it at home or in your pocket.

To learn more about your date, try doing a Google Search on your prospective date. To do a Google Search:

1. Open the Web browser on your computer.
2. In the address bar type in www.google.com.
3. In the Google Search window type in your date's name.
4. You may find many entries for that name. Make sure that you read about the person who is from your area and not someone from across the country.

WHERE SHOULD WE MEET ON
A FIRST DATE?

Going out on a first date can be stressful, at any age. Whether or not you know anything about your date, his/her friends or relatives, his/her job, you will want to play it safe.

Plan to meet in a public place that is well lighted and open with lots of people around. Never, never, get into his/her car or plan to meet him/her at their residence or hotel room, or any concealed location.

IS IT OKAY TO GIVE OUT MY EXACT ADDRESS?

You never have to give out your exact address. However, you do need to give a few clues to verify that you are from the area. At some point after the first or second date you may feel comfortable enough to give out your address.

WHAT IF MY DATE IS OVERLY INTERESTED IN MY FINANCIAL DETAILS?

Never, ever give out personal financial details. If someone is interested in your financial details, too soon, then cease contact with them immediately. Never send or give any money to anyone you have recently met.

There are some scam artists who prey on new daters, irrespective of age. Always be wary of people who seem more interested in your money than you!

DO I NEED TO TAKE MONEY ON A DATE?

Always take some cash with you — just in case you need it for cab fare or some other emergency. If you do not have a cell phone, take some coins for a pay phone.

Don't borrow money from your date. Be prepared!

SHOULD I TAKE A CELL PHONE WITH ME?

Yes. Before you leave on a date, make sure that your cell phone is fully charged. It is a good idea to preprogram it to speed dial a friend or the police.

Also, make sure your friends and family know your cell phone number.

If you do go to the movies, a play or anywhere that a ringing cell phone would be a disturbance, turn off the ringer of your phone.

WHAT IS THE APPROPRIATE ATTIRE FOR A DATE?

Dressing well makes a good first impression. It also helps keep you from sending mixed signals such as you want an intimate relationship immediately. Here are some hints about dressing for success on your date:

- Don't wear clothing that is too revealing.
- Wear clothing that is comfortable. If you don't feel good, you won't look good.
- Make sure that your clothing is clean. Make sure that your socks match, shoes, too!
- Wear appropriate attire for your planned activity.

IS IT OKAY TO HAVE AN ALCOHOLIC BEVERAGE ON A DATE?

Too much alcohol can weaken your defenses, cloud your judgment and it can leave a bad impression with your new friend. Plus, it's very unattractive.

Alcohol can loosen your inhibitions and allow you to let down your moral guard, so you end up doing things that you would never consider doing if you were sober.

If you decide to drink, make sure that you limit your intake.

WHAT IF MY DATE CONSUMES TOO MUCH ALCOHOL?

Do not prolong the date. Excuse yourself and go home alone. If you are concerned about leaving your date in that condition, talk to the establishment manager or call the police.

If you do drink, do so in moderation. Always avoid drinking and driving. Taxi cabs are cheap compared to a D.U.I. ticket or injuries sustained in a car wreck.

SAFE AND UNSAFE ACTIVITIES
FOR NEW ACQUAINTANCES

Play it safe when you are meeting someone for the first date. Try one of these suggestions:

- Meet for lunch.
- Meet for brunch.
- Meet for coffee.
- Meet for ice cream.
- Meet at a museum.

UNSAFE ACTIVITIES FOR
NEW ACQUAINTANCES

Until you get to know someone, arrange your meetings in public places. It is a bad idea to:

- Go for a drive to an unfamiliar place.
- Go to his or her home alone.
- Take a midnight walk on the beach.
- Take a hike in the woods.
- Spend a weekend in the country.

In summary — do not go anywhere you are totally alone with your new acquaintance.

SHOULD I TRUST MY INTUITION?

If you get that nagging feeling that something isn't right, trust your intuition. Get out of the situation. Better to be safe than sorry.

You do not have to finish any date and you never have to go out with them again, if you have a bad feeling about the person.

Listen to your inner voice.

WHAT IF MY DATE IS A HOT-HEAD?

A short-temper can be an indicator that this person has other problems. If your date suffers from lack of self-restraint, he or she could just as easily believe they are not responsible for their words or deeds, in the heat of the moment.

Just as bad as being a hot-head is a person who displays passive-aggressive tendencies.

Wide mood swings in a short period of time should raise a warning flag.

WHAT IF MY DATE IS TOO FORWARD?

If you feel uncomfortable with your date's physical or verbal advances and find that you can't deter them with subtle hints or outright admonitions — get away from this person, right away.

Intimacy should never be forced. It should be a mutual feeling. Be sure to voice your opposition if you feel uncomfortable with your date's behavior.

HAS DATING ETIQUETTE CHANGED OVER THE YEARS?

For the most part, dating etiquette has not changed over the decades. Good manners and chivalry never go out of style. Here is a list of good manners to consider:

- On a sidewalk, gentlemen properly walk nearest the street.
- Gentlemen rise when a lady enters the room.
- A gentleman will hold a door open for a lady to pass through. The lady should respond with a "thank you".
- When driving a car, the gentleman unlocks the door from the outside, helps the lady to her seat.
- A date in the passenger's seat should unlock the driver's door for the driver.
- At the movies, theatre or sporting events, the man allows the woman to walk ahead of him into the row; he sits on the aisle.
- When ordering dinner, the lady orders first.

ARE THERE ANY FOODS I SHOULD STAY AWAY FROM ON DATE NIGHT?

Until you get to know your date better, it is a good idea to stay away from certain foods. Here are a few to be weary of:

- Garlic/onion anything.
- Barbecued ribs.
- Spaghetti or pasta.
- Fried chicken.
- Oversized sandwiches and burgers.
- Poppy seeds.
- Whole lobster.
- Anything sloppy or that requires extra napkins!

WHAT ABOUT SEX ON THE FIRST DATE?

No way! You should spend some time getting to know your date rather than being confused by hormones. Plus, you need to talk about health issues ahead of time. Unless of course that's all you are looking for AND that's all they are looking for! If you do have sex on the first date, practice safe sex by using a condom.

PART 7

Sex and Love

Sex and love — two complicated subjects! As Seniors, you have the advantage of experience. This part is a quick review of things you probably already know, but maybe haven't thought about in a long time.

INTIMACY OF A KISS

A kiss can surpass sex as the most intimate form of expression. You can fake your way through sex, but a kiss tells all.

HOW CAN I BECOME A BETTER KISSER?

Kissing can run the gamut from sweet and romantic to hot and heavy. Remember these things:

- No bad breath.
- Do not lick your lips as you go in for the kiss.
- Your mouth is not a jack-in-the-box. Every time you open it, your tongue should not automatically pop out.
- Follow an orderly progression in any kissing session: closed mouth, opened mouth, no tongue, opened mouth, just a hint of tongue, full-on tongue probing.

THE "BEFORE SEX" TALK

Just because you are a Senior doesn't mean you shouldn't talk about STDs (sexually transmitted diseases) with your partner. Even though asking about STDs may seem awkward, it is necessary. Did you know that one out of every five individuals is carrying genital herpes, and most are not even aware of it?

Even if you have been in a monogamous relationship for most of your adult life, you need to be tested by a physician for STDs.

WHAT IF IT HAS BEEN A LONG TIME SINCE I HAVE HAD SEX?

By this age you should be much more comfortable with your sexuality. You know that sex is much more than intercourse. It is important that you voice your desires.

Things you already know:

- Nobody looks like a model when naked.
- Women need more time and stimulation as they grow older.
- Mutual orgasms are rare.
- Older men are at risk for erectile dysfunction. There are alternatives available.

There are many variations in arousal.

WHEN IS THE RIGHT TIME TO HAVE SEX?

Only you and your partner can answer that question. Things to consider:

- You've talked about it.
- You feel passionate about the other person.
- You have had more than four or five dates.
- You trust the other person.
- You know the other person's middle name.
- You are ready to have safe sex.
- You realize your fantasy may be greater than the sex itself.

WILL SEX CHANGE OUR RELATIONSHIP?

Because sex and emotion are linked together, becoming sexual partners may trigger powerful psychological and emotional dynamics.

Despite your intentions, it's quite possible you will fall in love, or at least develop a more serious relationship. Human beings, by nature, seek attachment and love even when not consciously aware of it.

WHAT IS CHEMISTRY?

Initially, chemistry is based on a visual attraction and reaction. Then reality sets in. If there is no initial chemistry, consider it a friendship more than a date.

Being attracted to a person isn't enough to sustain a healthy relationship over time, but it is necessary. Although it sounds contradictory, chemistry is an essential part of a healthy relationship.

IS IT LUST OR LOVE?

Good question. How can you tell? The love question has baffled singles for ages. How do you know if you lust or love a person in the beginning stages of a relationship? Love is very complicated. It's about trust and compatibility. It's about respect and acceptance. Here are some questions to ask yourself:

- Do you feel like calling your new friend all of the time?
- Do you kiss or touch every time you meet?
- Do you think about this person constantly?
- Is your connection primarily sexual?
- Do you *feel* in love?
- Is there chemistry and magnetism between you and your partner?
- Do you feel lucky to have each other in your lives?

If you do not have any other common values or mutual commitments your relationship may not last very long. It may just be lust.

WHY AM I STILL DATING YOU?

Your relationship should feel natural, easy and fun. It shouldn't feel predictable and boring.

Don't stay in a relationship just to avoid being alone. Don't settle for less than you deserve just to have someone.

Don't fall into the trap of feeling needed or responsible for another person's well being. Not only is it unfair to you, it is disrespectful to the other person.

ARE WE COMPATIBLE?

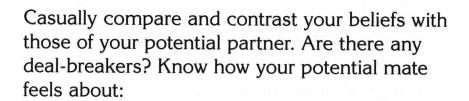

Casually compare and contrast your beliefs with those of your potential partner. Are there any deal-breakers? Know how your potential mate feels about:

- Religion.
- Marriage.
- Money.
- Lifestyle.
- Ethics and Morals.
- Politics.
- Commitment.

WHAT IF I'M LONELY BUT DON'T WANT TO GET MARRIED?

While some Seniors are looking to get married again, others just want the companionship that a relationship provides.

Many men and women were oriented in a "one person for life" philosophy. But there's that need (companionship) and the loneliness can be pervasive. There's a whole internal adjustment process of thinking about getting involved in another relationship.

The nice thing about dating when you are older is that you are more direct, you know what you want, and you mainly want to enjoy life with someone else!

MARRIAGE OR COMPANIONSHIP?

A lot of Seniors prefer companionship to marriage. There is a natural hesitancy to get involved in a new serious relationship, combine finances and risk having to take care of someone with a long illness.

The choice is yours.

Not everyone that you date will be marriage material, nor should they be, but they might be great dinner companions.

IS IT ALL RIGHT TO REMAIN SINGLE?

Yes. For some of you, the point of dating is not to find a partner, but to share experiences while remaining single. Maybe you have spent most of your life with a partner and now want to live out the next part without a partner. Be honest with your dates. (Don't be too hard on yourself if you change your mind.)

PART 8

Second, Third and Fourth Dates...

Okay, you've made it past the first date. Now what?

The second date denotes interest and the third date denotes even more interest.

The fourth date denotes deep personal interest. If you didn't kiss on the third date, now may be the time! Kiss with warmth. If it is mutual (obviously so) there may be some passion.

IS IT OKAY TO BE MORE NERVOUS ABOUT THE SECOND DATE THAN THE FIRST DATE?

More than likely you will be just as anxious about the second date as you were about the first date. Try to relax. At least you have a second date!

A second date is just another step in the process. You are still trying to figure out if you are compatible. The second date gives you another opportunity to start revealing who you really are.

HOW LONG SHOULD I WAIT BETWEEN THE FIRST DATE AND THE SECOND DATE?

One to two days, even though there are no set rules. Typically men tend to wait longer than women when arranging a second date. Keep in mind, they said yes because they liked you.

You might be able to gain some clues from the person if you see them in social situations such as club meetings or at the library. If the person smiles and flirts you probably could feel comfortable asking them out relatively soon.

However, if you are interested don't wait too long. The other person may take that as an insult. So, if you are sincerely interested in getting together, why wait?

WHAT SHOULD I EXPECT ON
THE SECOND DATE?

Be careful to not expect your date to think and feel as you do. Keep your expectations in perspective. Be aware of your own dating patterns. Do you quickly fall in and out of love or do you over analyze your dates to insure that you never find intimacy?

The more your interest has been aroused, the more important to find out if your date is leaning in the same direction. Unlike teens, older folks have had years of experience in partnership, life and also in sexual relations.

SHOULD WE TALK ABOUT
OUR PREVIOUS DATE?

Yes. It is a good conversation starter, especially if you had fun. Plus, it lets your date know that you were paying attention.

Bring up something they were interested in during your previous conversations. It gives you the chance to make corrections on any misunderstandings. However, don't rehash the same topic over and over. Try to keep the conversation fresh.

SHOULD WE GO TO A DIFFERENT PLACE ON THE SECOND DATE?

Yes. The location will reveal more clues about your date's personality. On your first ten dates it's better to vary what you do. Spend time together alone but also spend some of your time together getting to know each other's friends or family.

WHAT IF I AM HAVING TROUBLE GETTING A SECOND DATE?

If you are having trouble getting a second date, then ask yourself these questions:

- Did I make my date feel good about himself/herself?
- Was I interested in what he/she was saying?
- Did I laugh at his/her jokes?
- Did I compliment him/her in some way?

It is easy to get caught up in making a good impression. However, if your date feels important, special, smart, sexy, funny and good about himself/herself, then guess what? There's going to be a second and third date.

HOW TO KNOW IT'S MORE THAN
A PLATONIC FRIENDSHIP?

As you learn about each other, here are signs that things are moving ahead:

- The amount of time you spend together increases.
- You think about each other when you are apart.
- You feel comfortable sharing your feelings with each other.
- You express affection easily with each other.
- You listen attentively to each other.

TEN "GETTING TO KNOW YOU" QUESTIONS

Once you have gotten to know your date a little better and your comfort level is okay, you can begin to reveal more about yourself. Take turns answering these questions with your date:

1. If there were one food you could eat for a week, what would it be?
2. What is your favorite time of year?
3. What is your favorite flavor of ice cream?
4. Who is your best friend?
5. If you could fly anywhere for the day, where would you go?
6. Where do you see yourself in five years?
7. If I opened your closet right now what would I see?
8. What side of the bed do you sleep on?
9. What do you like the most about yourself?
10. What's the best present you ever received?

WHAT IF THE RELATIONSHIP IS GOING NOWHERE?

Sometimes it takes a couple of dates to realize that this person isn't the right person. If you are making all of the invitations or you only get together because you have nothing better to do, this may not be the right person. Other cautions include:

- You notice lies or inconsistencies in their stories.
- Dates are often broken.
- He/she doesn't ask about what you're doing.
- He/she doesn't want to meet any of your friends.
- There is no chemistry or spark between the two of you.

REVEALING INFORMATION:
WHEN AND HOW MUCH?

Getting to know each other is a process. However, too much information, too soon, can be a problem. Not revealing some information can be a problem, too.

Issues best to get out in the open:

- Previous marriages.
- Arrests and convictions.
- Money issues-bankruptcies.
- Children.
- Medical Issues.

THREE TIPS FOR SHARING FEELINGS

Sharing feelings can be tough. No one likes to feel vulnerable, which can easily happen if you open up. When sharing your feelings consider the following:

1. Start out slowly. Be cautious about what you say.
2. Think before you speak.
3. Gauge their reactions to what you say.

PART 9

Dealing With Rejection

Dealing with rejection is not fun. But it is a natural part of dating and meeting people. There are those who get over it faster than others. It is a good idea to conquer your fears of rejection before you start dating.

Most of the time rejection is a symptom of a "wrong fit". Something is not working for the other person. Sometimes rejection is a catalyst to make us change something about ourselves.

Tell yourself that it's their problem, not yours. If they don't want to go out with you, they're missing out.

HOW DO I COPE WITH REJECTION?

Rejection after a few dates is different from rejection from a relationship. If the rejection occurs after a few dates, keep your dignity and don't beg your date to give you another chance.

If you've developed a relationship with one of your dates, and they then reject you, surround yourself with your friends while giving yourself time to recover. Start looking for someone new with whom you can click.

WHAT IF I AM BEING REJECTED ON EVERY DATE?

If you get rejected on every single date, then it could be you. Re-evaluate your approach and appearance. Re-evaluate your table manners along with good manners in general.

Confide in a close friend and ask for an objective opinion.

WHAT'S THE BEST WAY TO REJECT SOMEONE?

When you are the one doing the rejecting, do it quickly and politely. You do not owe the person an explanation of why you are saying no. If they persist on asking why, blame it on yourself.

However, don't burn any bridges. You may change your mind in the future.

HOW DO I GET OVER BEING REJECTED?

They say if it doesn't kill you, it will make you stronger. Minimize your failure experiences and maximize your successes. Focus on your own personal growth and development. Resolve to be the best person you can be, to have the healthiest possible relationships. Then go out on another date.

WHAT ARE THE MOST COMMON DATING MISTAKES?

None of us is perfect and we've all made some dating mistakes. Here are some of the most common:

- I wish I had talked less and listened more.
- I wish I had been more open and lightened up.
- I wish I had been more honest about what I expect out of a relationship.
- I wish I had cooled my passions.
- I wish I had avoided making a foolish and impulsive decision.
- I wish I hadn't tried so hard.
- I wish I had dated more!

Learn from your mistakes and move on!

WHAT SHOULD I DO AFTER A
REJECTION OR BREAK-UP?

Seek out support from your family and/or friends.

Have supportive conversations with yourself and analyze what happened and learn from it.

Give yourself the necessary time to recover.

Start the dating process again.

PART 10

Online Dating

The Internet makes it easy for people from around the world to meet and become friends. The Internet also offers a number of computerized dating services. There is no longer a stigma attached to using a dating service. In fact, these days, it's cool to use a dating service. Everybody is doing it!

WHAT IS ONLINE DATING?

Online dating is just another way to meet other people. On your computer you can look for dates by interacting with others through e-mails, chat rooms and online dating services. Obviously the Internet does not provide the advantage of meeting people face-to-face, but it does have some advantages.

For example, you can look for dates 24-7 and from the comforts of your own home. You can also get to know someone before investing time and energy in going out. Ultimately though, on-line dating is a tool to get you a date.

WHY SHOULD I TRY ONLINE DATING?

There are several reasons you should give it a whirl:

- It is easy.
- It doesn't cost a lot of money.
- It saves you time.
- It is convenient. You can do most of it from the comforts of your home.
- There is a steady supply of potential dates.
- Online dating eliminates the awkwardness of first introductions.

WHAT DO I NEED TO GET STARTED IN ONLINE DATING?

You will need access to a computer. It is preferable to own your own computer so you don't have to worry about privacy issues as you would if you used a library computer or an Internet café computer.

You will need an Internet Service Provider (ISP): a company that connects your computer to the Internet. Your local cable, phone, or satellite company can provide you with more information.

You will also need an e-mail account. Email provides you a way to communicate to your potential dates you meet online.

WHAT IF I AM NOT A COMPUTER EXPERT?

That's okay. You do not have to be a computer whiz to try online dating. You do not even have to be a great typist. It is a simple process that almost everyone can do.

If you have not purchased and read *The Senior's Guide to Easy Computing*, then order it right now!

HOW DO I CHOOSE AN
ONLINE DATING SITE?

That is the sixty four thousand dollar question. There are thousands of sites to choose from. It is easy to feel overwhelmed. There are some ways to narrow down your search.

You can search for specific types of dating services, such as, Senior, African American, Baby Boomer, Hispanic, Jewish, Gay — whatever fits your specifics. You can search based on costs and services. There are lots of free sites available. There are plenty that offer a free trial period.

You can ask some of your friends which sites they recommend. You may be surprised at how many of your friends have tried an online dating service.

WHAT ARE THE ADVANTAGES
OF PAY SITES?

The old saying, "You get what you pay for" applies to fee-based dating sites.

Higher fees usually result in extra benefits and features. Here are some examples:

- Easy-to-understand directions.
- Limited Internet advertisements.
- Supervision to weed out the weirdoes.
- Require a minimum length for answers to essay questions.
- Supports photos of you.
- Allows payments by credit card.
- Approve of all postings.

WHY DO SOME PEOPLE USE FREE DATING SITES?

The main advantage of free sites is that they are free. However, dating sites must make revenue, which they do by selling advertising to other companies.

Here are some other characteristics of free sites:

- Inundated with advertising — pop-ups and banner ads.
- Not as much information about your prospects.
- Very little screening.

WHAT SHOULD I WATCH OUT FOR WHEN CHOOSING AN ONLINE DATING SITE?

If you do not want pornographic messages stay away from sites with "adult content".

Some sites require answers to all of the questions and others do not. If you do not have to say much about yourself, then it stands to reason, neither do your potential dates. You should be suspicious of someone who only lists a name and photo. Don't let your search turn into a photo contest.

Understand the site's privacy policy.

DO I HAVE TO HAVE A SPECIAL E-MAIL ACCOUNT?

You receive dating e-mails either in your personal e-mail account or in your e-mail account inside the dating site. (This type is called an all-in-one site.)

If you use a personal e-mail account, it is a good idea to create a new e-mail account that is dedicated exclusively to your online dating endeavors. There are plenty of places to get a free e-mail account (ex. Yahoo, Hotmail, MSN). The reason for setting up a separate e-mail account is for privacy purposes. So if your real e-mail address is johnwayne@aol.com you would not want to name your new account johnwayne@hotmail.com. Instead, come up with something less revealing. Remember, you only have to give out your real name and e-mail address when you are good and ready.

You may already have the capability to have multiple e-mail accounts with your ISP. Check it out.

DO I HAVE TO USE SPECIAL INTERNET JARGON?

No. However, you may run across some common dating-specific acronyms. Here are a few of the most common:

- LOL: Laughing out loud.
- ISO: In search of.
- SWF: Single white female.
- SBM: Single black male.

Set your search engine to Internet Acronyms to find a listing.

WHAT IS BLOCKING?

Blocking is an online feature that keeps others from knowing you are online. For instance, if you do not want potential dates to know that you are home on a Friday night, you could use this feature.

WHAT IS A CHAT ROOM?

A chat room is an online site for "chatting". There are two kinds of chat rooms — public and private. Discussions and conversations take place in real time and you can come and go as you please.

Most online dating chat rooms are defined by age. Typically chat rooms don't lend themselves to meaningful conversations.

WHAT ARE INSTANT MESSAGES (IM)?

It is a way for someone to jump into the corner of your online computer screen with a message, and try to engage you in a chat. IMs cannot come in if you're blocked. You can also go to your "buddy list" and block that person.

AOL has the most popular IM system called AIM. Best of all you don't need an AOL e-mail account to use their IM program. Check out www.AOL.com for more details.

DO I NEED A SCREEN NAME
AND A TAGLINE?

Yes.

Your screen name is like your nickname. Pick a good one because it is the first clue you give about who you are.

Many sites allow you to attach a phrase by your screen name. It's like a headline in a newspaper, used to get your attention. It should be fun and eye-catching. It should make someone want to read your profile.

WHAT IS A PROFILE?

A profile is your online resume. It usually consists of a few photos, answers to a basic questionnaire, followed by some essay questions.

Your profile is your way of introducing yourself to the world. Give some thought about what you want to say, and how to say it.

WHAT ARE SOME OF THE ROUTINE QUESTIONS FOUND ON MOST STRUCTURED SITES?

Even though each site is a little different, most sites ask the following:

- Age.
- Body type (weight).
- Children/Grandchildren.
- Drinking Habits.
- Education.
- Eye Color.
- Hair Color.
- Height.
- Income.
- Location.
- Marital Status.
- Occupation.
- Religion.
- Sexual Orientation.
- Smoking/Drug Habits.

FILLING OUT YOUR PROFILE: MARITAL STATUS

When filling out an application for an online dating site you are often asked about your marital status. Use the list below as a guide when answering the questions.

- **Single:** This option means you are not married now. It could also mean that you have never been married.
- **Divorced:** Being divorced is a legal matter and to some people this status does make a difference in their decision to date you.
- **Separated:** There are people who don't want to date someone who is separated, for fear they will go back to their spouse.
- **Widowed:** Most people don't lie about this option.

FILLING OUT YOUR PROFILE: AGE

Don't lie about your age even if you think you have a good reason for the deception.

By the way, most people who do lie about their age do so within five years of their true age.

Income:

There are several different schools of thought on this topic. You have two choices: give the true number or refuse to state your income.

Usually you can tell if a person is telling the truth by looking at their other answers/clues in their essays.

Religion:

How or if you answer this question depends on how important is your religious affiliation. Some sites give you the option of choosing spiritual or religious.

Smoking and Drinking Habits:

For some people these answers are deal breakers. Also, keep in mind, few people with drinking or drug problems are honest about their situation.

WHAT ARE THE ESSAY QUESTIONS LIKE?

Describe yourself. What are you looking for in a date?

Most essay questions are open-ended yet personal. The essay questions are easy because they are all about you.

If you do not answer the essay questions, you severely decrease your chances of finding a qualified date.

HOW DO I WRITE A GOOD ESSAY?

You don't have to be a genius to write a good essay. Use the following guidelines:

- Be honest.
- Don't forget, you're writing for an audience.
- Don't forget to have fun!
- Use lots of details.
- Use your spell-checker.
- Don't be negative, angry, sad or creepy.
- Grammar and proper punctuation count.

If you are having a difficult time answering the essay questions, ask a friend or relative to help you.

IS IT IMPORTANT TO HAVE A GOOD PHOTO?

It is one of the first things you see on the dating site and it's what draws you in. If you don't post a photo you will hardly be contacted by anyone at all. Not posting a photo also tends to raise suspicions.

Put up a picture that looks like you do today. (Resist the urge to put a photo that is several years old.) Your date will not appreciate false advertising.

Don't forget to smile!

HOW DO I GET MY PHOTO ONTO
THE DATING SITE?

You can e-mail a digital photo directly to the site. If you don't know how to use a digital camera you can read our book *The Senior's Guide to Digital Photography*.

If you don't own a digital camera yet, someone you know does. Ask your children, grandchildren or friends to help.

WHAT IS AUTO-MATCH?

The dating site takes most of your stats and matches you to others. (Essay questions are not used.) People new to online dating often start out using this feature. However, your odds of finding a compatible match are a lot better when you include the essay questions and answers.

WHAT IS WINKING?

A wink is an impersonal, standard message you can send via e-mail. Think of it as a wink of the eye. On some online dating sites, you can send a wink in response to a person's ad and photo. It requires no writing at all.

The person sending you a wink may have clicked on hundreds of other ads, including yours, and sent winks out to everyone, without singling your ad in any special way.

IS THERE MORE THAN ONE WAY TO FIND A MATCH ON A DATING SITE?

Yes. You can use one of the following approaches when finding your match on an online dating site:

1. You can be proactive and seek out matches. You make the first contact.
2. You post your profile and photo and let matches seek you out.

HOW DO I USE THE DATING SITE'S SEARCH ENGINE?

You need to be a real subscriber, not a trial member, to get access to it.

Most search engines do not include postings without photos, unless specifically selected.

Be aware of age bias. Some searches use age bands (65 to 75 years) instead of decades.

Many sites use zip codes and area codes as a way to formulate a person's location. The default distance is usually 50 miles. If you live in a big city, it may be necessary to change your zip code on your profile more toward the center of the city.

Check for new postings regularly.

Don't wait too long before sending an e-mail. Subscriptions expire.

WHY DON'T PEOPLE RESPOND
TO MY E-MAILS?

There are lots of reasons why you may not be getting the responses you want. Consider:

- The recipient doesn't like the way you look.
- The recipient doesn't like your essays.
- The recipient is new at online dating and is not sure what to do.
- The recipient is in a relationship but hasn't taken down their posting.
- The recipient hasn't paid their subscription fees but is still posted.
- The recipient is a moron. They should be responding to you. You're a great catch!

WHAT DO I DO AFTER I HAVE FOUND A MATCH?

Now it's time to write an introductory e-mail. Remember to keep it simple. Start with something relevant to the information in their profile. Talk about them, not you. Find a way to compliment them. Call them by their name.

Basically, in one paragraph, explain why you are writing to them instead of everyone else on the website. Stay away from form letters. Everyone wants to feel special.

Close with a warm salutation. Sign off using your real first name.

And remember, spelling, punctuation and proper grammar still mean something to most people.

HOW CAN I TELL IF MY MATCH IS BEING HONEST ?

It is easy for e-mail exchanges to become more personal, faster, than telephone or face-to-face exchanges would.

Don't project your fantasy onto the other person. Beware of rising and unreasonable expectations.

Pay attention to consistency. Many people are great at telling you what you want to hear in order to get a date. This could be a red flag.

Be cautious.

WHAT ARE THE TOP TEN ONLINE DATING SAFETY TIPS?

Most online safety tips are the same as traditional dating tips.

1. Use a separate e-mail account.
2. Use a cell phone number.
3. Do not give out personal information like your address.
4. When you meet for the first time, meet in a public place.
5. During the meeting be on alert for any discrepancies from previous correspondence.
6. Keep the meeting short.
7. Don't go to a second location during your first meeting.
8. Don't allow home pick-ups.
9. Don't give out any financial information.
10. Do a Google Search on their full name.

WHAT IS E-MAIL ETIQUETTE?

Etiquette is just as important in e-mail as it is in person. It is important to have good manners.

- Be honest.
- Ask top-priority, deal breaker-questions, first.
- Keep it light and simple.
- Be brief. Nobody wants to read an encyclopedia.
- Ask questions that require a little thought and writing instead of something that can be answered with yes, or no.
- Stay away from controversial subjects.

GIVING AND RECEIVING REJECTION

Rejection, to some degree, is a natural part of dating. Keep it in perspective. The beauty of online dating is that you have very little time and emotion invested in the contact.

Never be rude.

If you get rejected, move on. Remember, there are more fish in the sea. Don't take rejection personally. Your prospective date probably did you a favor by ending the email exchange.

HOW LONG DO I WAIT BEFORE MEETING IN PERSON?

It's a good idea to exchange several e-mails, at a minimum, before meeting in person. You should also have a few telephone conversations to make sure that you can communicate easily. There is no way of exactly knowing when to meet someone in person. Aim high. Choose wisely.

WHY IS THE INITIAL TELEPHONE CONTACT IMPORTANT?

Telephone contact is the second phase of online dating. You can tell a lot from a phone call. You can hear emotion (if they have any). You get instant feedback. Are they a quick thinker? Do they have a sense of humor?

TEN TELEPHONE TIPS

Most people don't realize that a phone call can make a big impression on what your date thinks of you.

1. Call when you say you are going to call.
2. Identify yourself (first and last name).
3. Speak clearly and slowly.
4. Don't belch, swear or interrupt.
5. Don't eat while you're on the phone.
6. Keep the call fairly short.
7. Be a good listener.
8. Be cheery and lively.
9. Take notes during the call.
10. Don't chew gum while talking on the phone.

WHAT IF I DECIDE I DON'T
LIKE ONLINE DATING?

Not a problem. Every dating site has a way to suspend or close an account. Before you suspend or resign, a good way to ensure that your account will be deleted is to delete your photo and essay answers. Then wait a few days and resign.

WHAT ARE POPULAR ONLINE DATING SITES?

There are hundreds of dating sites available. Three of the most popular are:

- SeniorSparks.com
- Match.com
- Yahoo! Personals

WHAT IS WWW.SENIORSPARKS.COM?

www.seniorsparks.com is an online dating site designed for senior citizens and specifically for those over the age of 65. Many of the other online sites for Seniors include people starting at age 50. Is a 50 year old really a Senior?

Go to your search engine and type in "dating sites" or "senior citizen dating sites". It will come up with thousands of sites. If you are new at online dating I would recommend going to www.seniorsparks.com.

The sign-up process is easy. www.seniorsparks.com doesn't offer a free online tour but it does offer free limited access (which is unlimited in length, but limited in function).

The www.seniorspark.com site also offers Senior Sparks Coffee Dates. In addition, the site features a page on dating tips, as well as, Ask Dr. Sparks (help) feature.

WHAT IF I'M JUST LOOKING FOR A NEW FRIEND?

A good starting place is www.meetasenior.com, a friendship site. The web site is similar to an online dating site, but the focus is on finding a like-minded friend rather than a date. If you are looking for a bridge partner, a fellow quilter, etc., this is a great place to start. Keep in mind there is a small subscription fee.

CONCLUSION

Dating is fun at any age. There are so many more avenues to meet new people than there were 50, 40, or even 20 years ago.

The time to start dating is right now. So, stick out your hand, flash them a smile and meet your new friend.

1. A coffee date for the first meeting is a good idea because it keeps the date at an hour or two. Also, these places are usually crowded, well lit, safe and perfect for meeting a stranger. Be practical, not cheap.

2. Cast a wide net.

3. Never give out personal financial details to anyone you have just met.

4. Trust your own instincts. If anything makes you uncomfortable, walk away for your own safety and protection.

5. Watch for red flags. Pay attention to displays of anger, intense frustration or attempts to pressure or control you. Acting in a passive-aggressive manner, making demeaning or disrespectful comments or any physically inappropriate behavior are all red flags.

6. Good conversation starters: Comment on his/her hobbies and interests. If you have children you will never run out of stories. Ask him/her about their favorite restaurant, recipe or food.

7. 35% of women prefer to date younger men.

8. It's okay to have dating as a lifestyle. Maybe you have spent the good part of your life with a partner, and you want to live the rest of it as a single person. That's fine, just be up front with your date that you are not trying to find another partner.

9. Good hygiene can mean the difference between a polite pat on the back and a night of love. Always take a bath or shower before your outing.

10. Visit www.DrRohm.com and take a personality assessment. The more you know about yourself the easier it will be to find a compatible date.

11. The power of a smile should never be underestimated. Use your smile as your secret weapon.

12. Do not approach or try to meet someone at any of the following places: a funeral, a crowded elevator, a dark alley, the XXX aisle of a video store.

13. Inappropriate questions to ask someone you just met: How much money do you make? What kind of car do you drive? How old are you?

14. In 2000, there were 14.4 million men and 20.6 million women aged 65 and over.

15. Skip the junk food. Good nutrition makes you feel better.

16. Flirting Tip: Whisper...it always gets their attention. Ask them if you can tell them a secret. Then whisper in their ear.

17. The most important part of flirting is to show interest in the other person.

18. Good table manners include: Chew your food with your mouth closed. Be polite to the waiters and staff. Tip well. Talk softly. Use your napkin.

19. It is okay to share an appetizer or dessert, but don't ask your date to split a meal with you.

20. If your date is going well, mention date number two before date number one is over.

21. Don't be late for your date. Everybody's time is valuable. Arriving late makes a poor impression. It shows selfishness and a lack of organization, and gets the date off on the wrong foot.

22. Be a good listener. When the talker says, "What are your thoughts on that?" it's embarrassing to have to ask that person to repeat what was just said.

23. Don't sound desperate. Statements like, *"This is my first date in 35 years"* might be a turnoff to someone who was otherwise interested in you.

24. Discussing politics or religion is risky. Most people don't like confrontation.

25. Nobody should have to walk on eggshells. If the relationship requires too much effort, it won't work.

26. Don't get stuck living in the past. Live in the present. Unload your baggage before you start dating.

27. There are many stereotypes about sexual expression and people with disabilities. If you are interested in dating someone with a disability, ask him/her out. Ask the person with the disability about accessible dating options.

28. Over 200 medications affect sexual performance and desire. Check with your physician.

29. Avoid premature sexual intimacy.

30. You are never too old to be at risk for HIV. In fact, the fastest growing AIDS rates are among people 50 and older.

31. Often on first dates, people forget to relax, laugh, smile and enjoy themselves.

32. Don't be so inflexible that you automatically dismiss someone who comes along but doesn't fit perfectly.

33. No matter what your age or social circumstance, you don't have to apologize for looking for the absolutely best partner for you.

34. Pursuing activities and interests we enjoy is more important than going out just to meet a date. People usually meet the partner of their dreams when they are not looking.

35. Look for someone whose values and standards match your own. A good companion is more important than how someone looks.

36. Being honest up front leaves time for more productive pursuits.

37. Often group events and reunions are better places to meet potential mates than singles functions, where the ratios are unfavorable and the environment is often too competitive.

38. You could be married tomorrow if you lowered your standards far enough. Don't. Better to wait for the real thing than to waste your time on something that won't last.

39. No amount of cosmetic dating will get the job done any better than good conversation will. An exchange of personal information, at a gradually deepening level of intimacy, and the sharing of some sort of pleasure are the critical elements of a date.

40. If your date compliments you don't just brush it off or say something rude about yourself. Say thank you. Do not put yourself down.

41. If you are concerned about topics of conversation, be sure to read a newspaper or watch a news program that day so you're up on world events.

42. Keep topics light and keep away from controversial issues on the first date.

43. Be open to your date's ideas about what to do on the date. Express yourself honestly and tactfully.

44. Thank the other person for the date, always without exception. Good manners never go out of style.

45. Focus on the other person. Pay attention to your date. No wandering eyes. No preoccupation with old relationships, world problems, etc. Be there.

46. Stay positive. Don't complain on a first date.

47. A first kiss should always be done while the two of you are alone. This will help to avoid any unnecessary nervousness and embarrassing situations.

48. Do not complain about dating.

49. Do not talk with your mouth full.

50. Do not answer your cell phone while at dinner.

51. Do not go out on a first date if you are sick. Reschedule.

52. Do not say that you feel like you have known your date forever.

53. Be realistic. Not everyone you date is going to love you. Some may not even like you!

54. You know the relationship is getting more serious when you no longer keep tabs of all the singles you know or date.

55. Resist making assumptions about your date's feelings and needs.

56. Refrain from using off color language or jokes, or making sexual references.

57. Differences in men and women's brains, account for some of the differences in communication styles.

58. You can be attracted to people who are like you. Opposites do attract, too.

59. When you are on a date, be sensitive to cues about whether you are getting along.

60. Someone you initially didn't find physically attractive can appear more attractive over time, as intimacy grows.

61. Trust but verify.

62. Eye contact is crucial when on a date. In communication, 55 percent is body language, 38 percent is intonation and seven percent is verbal.

63. Even if you don't like your date. Do not give him/her a hard time. Everyone deserves to be treated with respect.

64. Viewing a relationship in the beginning as a "maybe" is realistic and allows the time to discover true potential rather than getting caught up in the romantic illusion of an instant yes.

65. Remember, attraction is the fuel that runs the engine of a relationship. If there is absolutely no attraction in the beginning, the odds are against you in starting a committed relationship.

66. Intimate behavior repeated over and over with the same person leads to attachment, regardless of the suitability of the person.

67. Dating is a process. Be patient.

68. If you spend romantic time with the wrong person, you are setting yourself up for future heartache and frustration.

69. You have to know what you are looking for, before you can decide whether to stay or leave a relationship.

70. If your date likes what he/she sees, his/her lips will automatically part for a moment when your eyes first lock.

71. The raised brows, parted lips, flaring nostrils and wide eyes give the whole face a friendly "open" expression.

72. Preening gestures by men are equivalent to the female lip lick — "I want to look good for you."

73. When we first see someone we're attracted to, our eyebrows rise and fall. If they like us back, they raise their eyebrows. The whole thing lasts about one fifth of a second.

74. When on a date, if you rub your chin or touch your cheek, it indicates that you are thinking about you and her/him relating in some way.

75. To show your date that you are interested, speed up or slow down your speech to match hers/his.

76. If a guy pulls up or adjusts his socks in your presence, it's an almost 100 percent sign he's interested and trying to look his best.

77. Remember, dating as a Senior is much easier than dating as a teenager. You have much better social skills now. Get connected with other people who are in your situation.

78. If your date tells you, "You'd love my friend", it means he/she is not interested in you.

79. If your date says, "Can't we just be friends?" he/she is telling you there is no chemistry between you.

80. If you are dating someone in a major, different age bracket, be aware of the pitfalls that

can't always be predicted at the outset of the relationship.

81. Consider issues of health and wellness when taking on a new partner. Often age can and does make a difference.

82. Really listen to what your date has to say, and without judgment.

83. Don't let one bad date stop you from enjoying future dates.

84. Be on time. Lateness is inconsiderate (not to mention it reveals all sorts of things about your personality). If your date is late, be pleasant, and listen to their reason. It might be legitimate.

85. Never-ever send or give money to anyone you have recently met via a dating site. If they ask for money cease contact with them immediately.

86. Don't give complete trust to a likeable stranger. Get to know your date first.

87. Don't confuse sexual attraction with emotional bonding.

88. When a person calls for the first time after a few e-mails, do not stay on the phone for more than 20 minutes. The first call is to hear his/her voice, so that you know he/she is real, not to discuss their last three

relationships or yours, or his feelings about marriage. The first call is just to secure the date, a time and place for the meeting.

89. Online and offline, ask a lot of questions and watch for inconsistencies.

90. Beware of refusals to talk on the phone after establishing ongoing intimacy. Beware of evasive answers to direct questions.

91. Successful online dating requires a photo.

92. If you are looking for a friend, rather than a date, check out www.meetasenior.com

93. When signing up for online dating, beware of auto-debit when you give a credit card authorization for payment for your first subscription period. Be aware that you may be authorizing the site to automatically renew your subscription. Read the fine print.

94. If dating online, never mention in your first e-mail that you want to marry that person, or even date exclusively. Take your time.

95. Online dating is not therapy. Why are you dating? To deal with loneliness, vent anger, air dirty laundry, financial woes, and other misfortunes because you think this is a way to find sympathy, resolve issues, or bond. These are not reasons to date.

96. When online dating do not use special type-face, i.e., boldface, script, interesting color, etc. It screams that you are trying too hard.

97. If you have a friend who is also doing online dating, join the same service so you can see if the same people e-mail both of you and say the same thing.

98. Don't post a photo that doesn't represent your current appearance. Honesty is the best policy.

99. Over 99% of all people listed on Internet dating sites are sincere about finding a partner or new friend. However, there are still a few nuts out there. Be careful.

100. www.seniorsparks.com and www.meetasenior.com are popular social networking sites.

101. Be honest about what you are looking for from dating. Let your expectations work for you and not against you.

TERRIFIC WEB SITES

1. Senior Community
    www.theseniorsguide.com
2. Online dating for Seniors
    www.seniorsparks.com
3. Friend Locater
    www.meetasenior.com
4. Personality Assessment
    www.drrohm.com
5. Elder Law Answers
    www.McDermott.elderlawanswers.com
6. AARP
    www.aarp.org
7. Council on Aging
    www.ncoa.org
8. Dating Information
    www.ivillage.com
9. Governmental Resources
    www.firstgov.org
10. National membership of professionals who
    work with Seniors
    www.asaging.org
11. Resources
    www.about.com
12. Travel and Culture
    www.cntraveler.com
13. Food and Drink
    www.epicurious.com

TERRIFIC WEB SITES

14. Bridge
    www.bridgeworld.com

15. Pen Pals Around the World
    www.writeseniors.com

16. Electronic Greeting Cards
    www.bluemountain.com

17. Send flowers
    www.1800flowers.com

18. Elder hostels
    www.elderhostels.org

19. Travel
    www.advancedseniorsolutions.com

20. Resources
    www.seniorcitizensbureau.com

21. Poetry
    www.lovepoemsandquotes.com

22. Chocolates
    www.godiva.com

23. Information
    www.seniorjournal.com

24. Health & Fitness-seniors
    www.dmoz.org

25. Baby Boomer Headquarters
    www.bbhq.com

INDEX

INDEX

Check out these other great titles in the Senior's Guide Series!

The
Senior's Guide
to Digital Photography

The
Senior's Guide
to Easy Computing

The
Senior's Guide
to eBay®